Young Naturalist
Field Guides

Wildflowers, Blooms, and Blossoms

by Diane L. Burns

illustrations by Linda Garrow

Gareth Stevens Publishing
MILWAUKEE

DEDICATION

To my nieces, Heather, Amanda, and Kelly, three lovely flowers of young womanhood.
Bloom and flourish, dear hearts.

ACKNOWLEDGMENTS

Grateful thanks to Rhinelander High School botany teacher, Dawn Bassuener; at Hanson's
Rhinelander Floral Company, Karen Stroede; Jill Burns, Karen Sackett, Bonnie Kofler, and
especially the Hempels — Ruth and Henning — of Forth Floral.

**For a free color catalog describing Gareth Stevens Publishing's list of high-quality
books and multimedia programs, call 1-800-542-2595 (USA) or
1-800-461-9120 (Canada). Gareth Stevens Publishing's Fax: (414) 225-0377.**

Library of Congress Cataloging-in-Publication Data

Burns, Diane L.
    Wildflowers, blooms, and blossoms / by Diane L. Burns; illustrated by
Linda Garrow.
       p. cm. — (Young naturalist field guides)
    Includes bibliographical references and index.
    Summary: Identifies twenty-eight popular wildflowers, where they can be
found, and what creatures eat them.
    ISBN 0-8368-2148-3 (lib. bdg.)
    1. Wildflowers—Juvenile literature. 2. Wildflowers — Identification—
Juvenile literature. [1. Wildflowers. 2. Wildflowers—Identification.]
I. Garrow, Linda, ill. II. Title. III. Series.
QK49.B94   2000
582.13—dc21   99-049626

This North American edition first published in 2000 by
Gareth Stevens Publishing
1555 North RiverCenter Drive, Suite 201
Milwaukee, Wisconsin 53212 USA

Based on the book, *Wildflowers, Blooms and Blossoms,* written by Diane L. Burns, first
published in the United States in 1998 by NorthWord Press, 5900 Green Oak Drive,
Minnetonka, MN 55343, Creative Publishing International. © 1998 by
Diane L. Burns. Illustrations by Linda Garrow. Book design by Russell S. Kuepper.
Additional end matter © 2000 by Gareth Stevens, Inc.

Printed in Mexico

1 2 3 4 5 6 7 8 9 04 03 02 01 00

CONTENTS

Wildflowers, Blooms and Blossoms

Metric Conversion Table

1 inch = 2.54 centimeters
1 foot = .3048 meter

INTRODUCTION

Wildflowers are plants that grow freely. People do not choose where flowers grow in the wild. The plants do.

So, wildflowers grow in many different kinds of places. They are found in many colors, sizes and shapes. Some are beautiful. Some are plain-looking. Some smell good. Others do not.

Some wildflowers are native to North America. Early settlers brought others to the area, either on purpose or by accident.

Wildflowers have many kinds of seeds. Some are food for wildlife. The whole plant, or parts of it such as flowers, roots and leaves may also be food for certain birds and other animals.

This *Young Naturalist Field Guide* and its activities will help you find some interesting wildflowers. Use the ruler on the back of the book to measure what you discover. Bring a pencil and paper along to draw what you see.

Have fun exploring the world of *Wildflowers, Blooms, and Blossoms!*

COMMON BUTTERCUP

WHAT IT LOOKS LIKE

Common buttercups grow to 3 feet tall and have many fuzzy branches.

The plant has two kinds of leaf stems and leaves. On the top, the small, three-part leaves have short stems or no stems at all. On the lower part of the plant, the leaf stems are long and each leaf is bigger and shaped like a skinny hand.

This wildflower's name comes from the delicate yellow cups that form the flowers. They are shallow, shiny, and about 1 inch across. Each flower has five overlapping petals that grow at the end of long, slender stems. It blooms from May through October.

INTERESTING FACTS

Because the plant can be poisonous to livestock, they avoid it.

WHERE TO FIND IT

The common buttercup likes wet meadows, swamps and road-sides. It grows in the western states, across the Plains states and to the Atlantic Coast.

Other kinds of buttercups grow in the south and central United States.

WHAT EATS IT

Ducks, wild turkeys and snow buntings eat buttercup seeds. Deer, muskrats and skunks eat the plants.

Wear boots and other protective clothing.

WHITE TRILLIUM

WHAT IT LOOKS LIKE

This wildflower has three white, triangle-shaped petals with wavy edges. Other kinds of trilliums have red, purple or yellow-green flowers. Each petal is about 3 inches long.

All trillium leaves grow in three's that look like smooth, dark green triangles. Each leaf is about 3 inches wide and 6 inches long.

This plant grows to 18 inches tall. It likes shaded, moist woods where it isn't bothered.

WHERE TO FIND IT

White trilliums grow from Minnesota and the Central Plains east to New England and south to Virginia. Other kinds of trillium grow along the eastern edge of the prairies and from Washington south to California.

White trilliums bloom in late spring. If you see a pink one, don't be fooled. After the white trillium's blossom has been open for a few days, it begins to turn pink.

WHAT EATS IT

Certain types of flies like the flowers, but probably not because of the smell. White trilliums have only the faintest of fragrance, and many others don't smell pleasant at all.

INTERESTING FACTS

Trillium is nicknamed "wake-robin," because it is said to wake the robins in the spring.

Please treat all wildflowers gently.

WILD LARKSPUR

WHAT IT LOOKS LIKE

Larkspur grows from less than 1 foot, to 8 feet tall, depending on the type.

The plant looks lacy because each larkspur leaf has several deep, finely cut sections. It looks like a skinny green hand.

The small flowers are often blue, but can also be white, pink or purplish with a pale center. Each flower has 5 petals. There is a long spur that sticks up from the top petal. They seem to nod gently as they bloom from spring, through summer and into fall.

The blossoms have a faint fresh scent.

WHERE TO FIND IT

Larkspur is found in woods and on slopes in much of the United States, especially in the Midwest and East. Shorter kinds grow in open, windy places. Taller ones grow in sheltered, moist places.

WHAT EATS IT

Hummingbirds like the flowers. It is harmful to cattle.

SPECIAL WARNING

Caution! The seeds, which grow in the center of the flower, are poisonous.

INTERESTING FACTS

Some kinds of larkspur bloom high in the mountains—above 10,000 feet!

TURK'S-CAP LILY

WHAT IT LOOKS LIKE

This sturdy wildflower grows to 8 feet tall! The upright stems are purplish. The narrow, sword-shaped leaves are about 5 inches long. They grow in groups along the stem.

Several orange-red flowers, speckled with brown spots, may grow at the end of the branch. They look graceful because the ends of the petals curl backward almost to the stem.

Turk's-cap petals are up to 3 inches long and less than 1 inch wide. At the base, each one is green, then yellowish spotted with brown, and orange-red at the tip.

WHERE TO FIND IT

The turk's-cap lily is found in the wet meadows and swampy woods of the eastern United States, west to the edge of the Great Plains.

It likes to be sheltered from harsh sun and wind. Look for it in July and August. One flower can bloom for a whole month. It does not have a smell.

WHAT EATS IT

Hummingbirds like the flowers.

Interesting Facts

Their appearance, which looks like a middle-eastern hat, gives the flower its name.

Take your time and don't hurry.

BLACK-EYED SUSAN

WHAT IT LOOKS LIKE

The plant grows to 3 feet tall on straight, stiff stems. Its few branches have fine hairs on them.

Black-eyed Susan leaves are thick, coarse and narrow. The bottom leaves, which are longer than the top ones, may be 2 inches wide and 7 inches long.

A single flower, up to 4 inches across, grows at the end of a stem or branch. Each flower has 12 or more bright yellow petals about 2 inches long. The center is a cone that looks like a big brown gumdrop.

WHERE TO FIND IT

This wildflower and its relatives are sun-lovers. They thrive in dry meadows, pastures, roadsides and vacant lots across the United States.

It blooms from May through September and has a faint, sweet smell.

WHAT EATS IT

Cattle and sheep eat this wildflower.

INTERESTING FACTS

The Black-eyed Susan gets its name from the big, dark center in each flower.

Use the ruler on the back of this book to measure what you find.

PURPLE CONEFLOWER

WHAT IT LOOKS LIKE

The purple coneflower grows from 1 to 3 feet tall on a stout, hairy stem. There are only a few branches, if any.

Its narrow leaves are up to 6 inches long and 3 inches wide. They feel coarse and are hairy.

Purple coneflowers are huge drooping flowers. They grow up to 6 inches wide, at the tips of the stems and branches. Coneflower petals can be 3 inches long. They are found in bright purple, red, pink and white.

WHERE TO FIND IT

The purple coneflower isn't fussy. It likes deep, moist soil, and can also grow in a dry, sunny spot. Look for it in the fields and meadows of the Midwest, and from Pennsylvania to Georgia, west to Oklahoma and north to Minnesota.

The flowers bloom from June to October, filling the air with their sweet scent.

WHAT EATS IT

Goldfinches love these seeds!

Sit quietly and you will see what kinds of wildlife also enjoy wildflowers.

BLOODROOT

WHAT IT LOOKS LIKE

This fragile plant grows no more than 1 foot tall on a smooth stem.

Each leaf looks hand-shaped and is about the same size. It is always curved with the whitish underneath part facing you.

A single white flower grows on a long stem separate from the leaves. It is as wide as 1-1/2 inches with a yellow center, and has as many as 16 petals. The white bud is often hidden inside the leaves, so you must look carefully to see it.

WHERE TO FIND IT

You will find bloodroot growing throughout much of the United States, especially in the Atlantic coastal states south to Florida, and west to Nebraska and Minnesota.

They bloom in rich shady woods from March to May, with no fragrance.

WHAT EATS IT

Bloodroot and ants help each other. Bloodroot's seeds are ant food. And bloodroot plants spread to new places because the ants carry the seeds with them.

SPECIAL WARNING

Caution! The juice is harmful. Do not swallow it!

BUTTER-AND-EGGS

WHAT IT LOOKS LIKE

Butter-and-eggs plants grow to 2-1/2 feet on thin stems that bend easily.

Soft, needle-shaped leaves, about as long as your finger, stick out along the length of the stem.

The showy yellow flowers blossom in a spike along the upper end of the branches. Each flower in the spike is about 1 inch long and looks like a set of small yellow lips with an orange center.

INTERESTING FACTS

This wildflower sounds like it might be someone's breakfast. But its name comes only from the flowers' coloring. The yellow outsides are the butter; the orange centers are the eggs.

WHERE TO FIND IT

Throughout the United States, butter-and-eggs grow in dry places, like vacant lots, where they often form large patches.

WHAT EATS IT

The many flowers on the butter-and-eggs plant bloom from July through October but their smell isn't pleasant. Still, bumblebees and some beetles like the pollen.

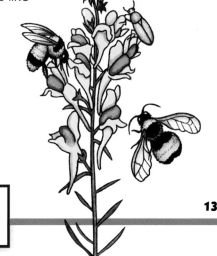

Tell an adult how long you will be gone.

CANADA THISTLE

WHAT IT LOOKS LIKE

Canada thistle plants can grow more than 4 feet tall. The straight, woody stems have slender green grooves in them.

Its narrow leaves can be longer than your hand. They have sharp spines.

Canada thistle flowers are purple, pink or yellow-white puffballs at the top of a green ball. They grow at the ends of the branches.

Each puffy flower, less than 1 inch wide, blooms all summer long and into autumn. They are very fragrant.

WHERE TO FIND IT

This wildflower could be nicknamed "survivor."

It is found across the United States almost everywhere a plant can grow.

In good conditions, it forms large patches in sunny vacant lots, meadows and overgrown fields.

WHAT EATS IT

Canada thistle is a special plant to goldfinches, which feed their young on the immature fruit. They also line their nests with the down from the flowers.

Bees and painted lady butterflies like Canada thistle flowers. Antelopes eat the whole plant. Goldfinches, sparrows and chickadees eat the mature seeds.

INTERESTING FACTS

Long ago, people thought thistle was a charm against deadly disease.

SPECIAL WARNING

Caution! Be careful of the sharp spines.

14

LATE GOLDENROD

WHAT IT LOOKS LIKE

Goldenrod blooms in an arch along the upper side of a short branch. About a dozen tiny yellow flowers form each arch. Look for them in late summer and early autumn and sniff for their sweet smell.

You might get a stiff neck finding this wildflower. Late goldenrod grows on a smooth, straight, purplish green stem that can be 8 feet tall!

Goldenrod leaves are narrow. They can be smooth on both sides, or hairy underneath. They grow along the stem and are about 6 inches long and 1 inch wide.

WHERE TO FIND IT

This is one of more than a hundred kinds of goldenrod that grow almost everywhere in the United States, in moist, sunny meadows.

Want to see next year's goldenrod now? Look in autumn, at the bottom of this year's goldenrod plant. You will find next year's stems already beginning to grow.

WHAT EATS IT

Flies, skippers and other butterflies like the flowers. Prairie chickens, rats and rabbits eat the leaves.

INTERESTING FACTS

Some kinds of goldenrod have latex in the leaves which scientists think may be a future source of rubber.

Take this book and a pencil when you go exploring.

Make a Wildflower Paperweight

Would you like to keep your favorite wild blossom? Make a wildflower paperweight! Besides keeping a pile of papers in place, the paperweight will keep your memory of sunny blooming meadows all year long.

something to do

WHAT YOU NEED
▼

- A clean, smooth, fist-sized rock
- A freshly picked wildflower blossom, with or without its stem and leaf
- A bottle of white glue
- Hairspray or spray shellac

WHAT TO DO
▼

1 Lay your wildflower wrong side up.

2 Carefully dab bits of white glue onto the back of the flower.

3 Paste the flower, right side up, to the rock. Work carefully, so the flower does not tear.

4 Allow the glue to dry before spraying the flower and the rock with hairspray or shellac. Be careful not to spray yourself!

5 Allow the spray to dry before you handle the paperweight.

You can display your creation in a favorite place, or give it as a gift.

Make a Friendship Band

Around the world, a gift of wildflowers has long been a symbol of friendship and trust. You can continue the tradition by making a wildflower friendship band.

WHAT YOU NEED
▼

- Long, freshly picked stems of wildflowers such as White Clover, Black-eyed Susan, Ox-eye Daisy, Indian Paintbrush, Orange Hawkweed, Butter-and-Eggs, Late Goldenrod, Evening Lychnis or Queen Anne's Lace.
- You can use the stems with or without the leaves and flowers attached.

If you use very fresh, green stems, your friendship band may last several days.

WHAT TO DO
▼

1 Tie together three stems of approximately the same length.
2 Gently braid the stems together.
3 When you reach the other end, tie it carefully.
4 Hold the braid around your wrist, ankle or forehead.
5 Tie it into a circle at the proper length.

Your plant band is much like the ones long-ago people wore on special occasions. You can keep it, or give it to a friend.

CORNFLOWER

WHAT IT LOOKS LIKE

Cornflower plants grow to about 2 feet tall. The stems are slender, grooved and branched. The many gray-green leaves can be woolly when young. They look like grass and are about 6 inches long.

Each flower is really a cluster of mini-flowers with the ones on the outer edge bigger than the center ones. They have deeply toothed edges.

The round flower blooms at the end of each branch. It is between 1 and 2 inches wide and tall. It is usually deep bright blue, but can also be purple, pink or white.

WHERE TO FIND IT

Cornflowers like fields, vacant lots and roadsides from New England south to Virginia and west across the United States to the Pacific Northwest.

Cornflowers, which do not have a smell, bloom in late summer and early autumn.

WHAT EATS IT

Wildlife do not usually eat the cornflower.

INTERESTING FACTS

This wildflower's nickname is "bachelor's button" because the blossom's ragged edges once reminded people of the frayed cloth buttons worn by "helpless bachelors."

Visit your favorite wildflowers in different seasons to see how they grow and change.

WHITE CLOVER

WHAT IT LOOKS LIKE

White clover stems may be up to 3 feet long, but they grow along the ground. Runners send down roots at each joint. The stems on which leaves and flowers grow are only about 5 inches tall.

Small and green, clover leaves always grow in groups of three or sometimes four. Each has a pale triangle across it. The leaves grow on stems separate from the flowers.

White clover flowers are small white to pink-white globes that bloom from May to December. They have a sweet smell.

WHERE TO FIND IT

Some type of white clover is found growing nearly everywhere in the United States, in lawns and fields and along roadsides.

WHAT EATS IT

Sulphur butterflies especially like clover flowers. Deer, squirrels, marmots, rabbits and grouse eat white clover leaves.

INTERESTING FACTS

Many people think four-leaf clovers are lucky. This idea started long ago when people believed that whoever found one would be able to see witches.

To see small plants more easily, carry a plastic magnifying glass with you.

WILD ROSE

WHAT IT LOOKS LIKE

This wildflower grows from 1 to 5 feet tall on straight stems that often have prickles. The plant can look slim or bushy, depending on what kind of wild rose it is and where it is growing.

Rose leaves are small, oval and dark green. Several stems usually grow into a bush.

The flowers can be as big as the palm of your hand. They are pink, white, yellow or red and grow singly or in a cluster. Each flower has a yellow center.

Its thorny patches make good hiding places for many animals, such as rabbits, mice and grouse. Wild rose bushes even make good homes for birds like cedar waxwings and chipping sparrows that nest in the thorny branches.

WHERE TO FIND IT

The wild rose likes sunny dry places such as rocky roadsides, fencelines and pastures. It grows almost everywhere in the United States.

It blooms from June to September. You can find the flowers by the strong, sweet smell.

WHAT EATS IT

Birds, grouse, quail, wild turkeys, squirrels, mice, bears, mountain sheep, opossums, and coyotes eat the fruit, called hips. Deer and antelope eat the twigs and leaves. Rabbits chew the buds and bark. Bees like the flowers.

INTERESTING FACTS

Rose hips, which have more vitamin C than oranges, can be found on the bush all winter.

Watch where you step.

BUSHY ASTER

WHAT IT LOOKS LIKE

The bushy aster grows to about 3 feet tall. The stems are widely branched, slender and tough. The green leaves are about as long as your finger and very narrow.

Bushy aster flowers grow in clusters. Each one is small, about 1/2 inch across, with thin, narrow petals. The flowers are blue-white to white, with yellow centers.

The flowers bloom in late summer and early fall without a smell. They can even be found on the plant after the first snowfall.

Other kinds of aster grow in almost any kind of soil, from rocky to boggy, and are found across the United States.

WHAT EATS IT

Some kinds of wild aster are good food for elk and deer. Other kinds make some animals sick. Bees, flies and butterflies like the flowers.

Interesting Facts

The bushy-looking top gives the plant its name. Some kinds of aster grow to 8 feet tall.

WHERE TO FIND IT

The bushy aster grows across the eastern and midwestern United States, in sandy soil.

Never pull up wildflowers by the roots. They cannot grow back.

MARSH MARIGOLD

WHAT IT LOOKS LIKE

This wildflower grows to 2 feet tall on thick, smooth stems.

Marsh marigold leaves are dark green and heart-shaped. They are smooth, from 2 to 8 inches wide.

These flowers have no special smell. They are bright yellow and shaped like a waxy shallow cup. Each one is less than 2 inches across. The centers are yellow-green.

The flowers open and close with the sun while they bloom from April to June.

WHERE TO FIND IT

This plant likes wet areas. It is found in swamps, marshes and ditches with slow-moving or standing water.

Marsh marigolds grow throughout New England and the East Coast, south to South Carolina and west to Nebraska. They are also found on the West Coast.

WHAT EATS IT

No wildlife eats this plant because it is harmful to them.

INTERESTING FACTS

Marsh marigolds were once used as a sign of spring. Long-ago people hung bunches of the wildflower over their doorways on May Day.

SPECIAL WARNING

Caution! Don't eat this plant! It can make a person sick.

WILD BLUE FLAG

WHAT IT LOOKS LIKE

This plant grows to 3 feet tall. Its stems are straight and may have a branch or two that reach upward.

The blue flag's leaves are narrow, like an upright sword.

Its flowers often grow two to a stem. They are violet-blue, with streaks of yellow, white and green. Several slender petals curve gracefully downward. Each one is about 4 inches long.

WHERE TO FIND IT

This wildflower grows along the marshy edges of meadows, and open wet brushland that is sunny. Look for it among other wet-loving plants, not in a patch by itself.

One kind or another of blue flag grows nearly everywhere in the United States. They bloom from May to July.

WHAT EATS IT

The leaves provide hiding places for wild ducks and geese, but the wild flag plant is not a source of food for wildlife. However, hummingbirds do like the flowers, which have a faint, fresh scent.

INTERESTING FACTS

The root of one kind of blue flag is used to make perfume.

Never collect rare or endangered wildflowers.

FIREWEED

WHAT IT LOOKS LIKE

Fireweed flowers grow in a spikelike cluster. Each flower in the cluster is about 1-1/2 inches across, with 4 rounded petals and a bright, rosy-purple color. Unopened buds droop downward.

This wildflower can grow to 8 feet, although most are 3 to 5 feet tall. Each stem is straight and strong. It can be smooth or have a fine downy covering. It is branched or unbranched.

Fireweed leaves are dark green on top, pale green underneath. They are pointed, and each is about 6 inches long and 1 inch wide.

WHERE TO FIND IT

Fireweed is found in the United States from New England to South Carolina and west to California and Alaska. It also grows from the Rocky Mountains south into Arizona.

The flowers bloom in summer months, with the lower flowers on the plant blossoming first.

Look for it in open areas and along sunny roadsides.

WHAT EATS IT

Although the flowers have no smell, hummingbirds and bees like them. Deer and moose eat the plant. Chipmunks eat the seeds.

INTERESTING FACTS

Fireweed got its name because it likes to grow in places after a fire. And from a distance, fields of open blooms look as if they are on fire.

Take sunscreen with you, and water to drink.

QUEEN ANNE'S LACE

WHAT IT LOOKS LIKE

This wildflower grows 4 to 5 feet tall on a strong, slender stem. The leaves are feathery and look like carrot tops.

Each large flower is made up of many smaller ones. The large blossom can be 4 inches wide, and up to 2 inches thick. It is white and can have a purple or reddish flowerette in the center.

The flowers of Queen Anne's Lace take two years to bloom. The first year, there are no flowers, only a circle of ferny leaves and its root. In the second year, the plant blooms between June and September.

After it blooms, the flower folds inward into a "nest" that shelters the plant's fruits. Look for this in early autumn.

WHERE TO FIND IT

Queen Anne's Lace is a common wildflower in sunny places like roadsides, vacant lots and fields. Though it is more common in the eastern United States, it can be found from coast to coast.

WHAT EATS IT

Sweet-smelling Queen Anne's Lace flowers are enjoyed by bees, butterflies, moths and flies. Its seeds are food for moles and grouse. Moles also eat the roots.

INTERESTING FACTS

Queen Anne's Lace is a kind of wild carrot. Long ago, when people dug them up, finding a forked root was considered lucky.

SPECIAL WARNING

Caution! Some people's skin is sensitive to touching the wet leaves of Queen Anne's Lace.

25

Ox-Eye Daisy

WHAT IT LOOKS LIKE

Ox-eye daisies can grow to 3 feet tall. The green, straight stem is smooth and usually unbranched.

Its narrow leaves can be 3 inches long. They are dark shiny green.

Each flower, up to 2 inches wide, grows at the end of a branch, one to a stem. There are 20 to 30 flat white petals, usually with a dent or two in the end of each petal. The flower's yellow center is depressed in the middle, like a thumbprint.

common in the West and South. These daisies like sunny roadsides, pastures and fields.

They have no smell, and bloom from May through November.

WHAT EATS IT

Wildlife do not usually eat the ox-eye daisy.

WHERE TO FIND IT

Ox-eyes grow from coast to coast, though they are less

26

PICKERELWEED

WHAT IT LOOKS LIKE

Pickerelweed can grow to 4 feet tall. Its thick, dark green leaves are smooth, wide, and shaped like spears. They grow up from the base and can be 10 inches long and 6 inches wide.

Pickerelweed often forms a thick, matted bed of leaves and flowers.

This wildflower gets its name because it often grows at the edge of water in which the pickerel fish is found.

The pale blue to deep violet flower spike is about 4 inches long. It grows at the end of a thick stem. The flower clump is crowded with small, individual flowers that have no smell.

WHERE TO FIND IT

Look for pickerelweed along the edges of shallow ponds, streams, rivers and bayous. Pickerelweed blooms all summer and into early fall.

It grows throughout the eastern United States west to Minnesota and south to the Gulf of Mexico, Florida and Texas.

WHAT EATS IT

The seeds are food for ducks and deer. The plant is food for muskrats.

Never step into water without first knowing how deep it is.

Preserve a Wildflower

Fresh blooms and blossoms wilt and fade once they are picked. Pressing each one to remove moisture preserves them much longer.

- A freshly picked wildflower with a flat blossom, such as buttercup, daisy, cornflower, wild rose or bushy aster. (Thicker blooms do not press well.) You can leave the stem and a leaf attached.

- 2 flat, smooth bricks (or big and heavy books)

- 2 pieces of waxed paper cut to fit the size and shape of the bricks or books

- 2 pieces of paper towel to fit the size and shape of the bricks or books

WHAT TO DO

▼

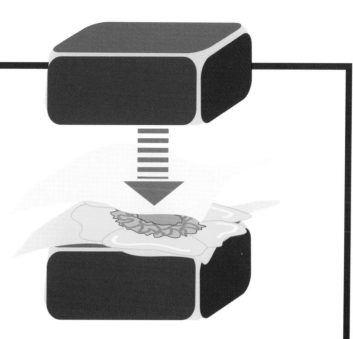

1. Lay a piece of waxed paper on top of one brick (or book). Then lay a piece of paper towel on top.
2. Next, place the wildflower.
3. Put the second piece of paper towel on top of the flower. Then lay the second piece of waxed paper over it all.
4. Finally, lay the second brick or book on top of your "sandwich."
5. Leave the whole "sandwich" alone for a few weeks while the flower dries and is pressed by the weight of the bricks.
6. Then, carefully take off the top brick or book.
7. Peel away the waxed paper and paper towel from both sides of the pressed wildflower.

You can keep the pressed flower as a memento in a favorite book or use it to make other things.

Here are some ideas:

- Glue it to plain paper and make your own sheets of wildflower stationery.
- Glue it to plain folded paper and make your own greeting cards.
- Press it between strips of clear tape to make a bookmark.
- Press it between strips of clear tape to make a suncatcher, and hang it in your window.
- Glue it to a safety pin for a beautiful piece of jewelry.

Pressed and preserved wildflowers make great gifts!

WILD COLUMBINE

WHAT IT LOOKS LIKE

Wild columbine is a short, lacy-looking bush that can grow 2 feet tall.

Its dark green leaves have deeply cut edges and grow in groups. They are lighter green underneath. Each leafy group can be as wide as 8 inches.

Each blossom is a drooping red and yellow bell. It nods at the end of the stem and is 1 to 2 inches long. The flower looks like a hollow, round honeycomb with 5 long spurs behind.

It blooms from April through July.

shade along rocky cliffs, fields and fencelines.

This wildflower is found across the eastern and central United States, south to Florida and Texas, and into the Rocky Mountains.

WHAT EATS IT

Even though this flower is not fragrant, it is a favorite of moths and butterflies.

INTERESTING FACTS

Sometimes bumblebees steal the sweet nectar without touching the flower to pollinate it.

WHERE TO FIND IT

Columbines like rich woods and loose soil. Look for them growing in light

Stay safe! Don't go near the edges of cliffs and outcroppings.

CHICORY

WHAT IT LOOKS LIKE

Chicory plants grow to 4 feet tall and look bare. The tough clump of hollow stems is hairy and branched. The stems start out green, turn purple, then red and finally brown as summer ends.

The few, skinny leaves along the stem can be 6 inches long. They have deep cuts in the edges and are gray-green. Most of the leaves grow in a circle at the base of the stem.

Chicory's flowers bloom along the upper stems. Each head is about the size of a quarter. Several flowers may be clustered together, right against the stem. They are usually blue, but they can also be pink or white.

The tips of the petals are square with notches. Each flower looks fringed and has no smell.

WHERE TO FIND IT

Chicory likes sunny fields, roadsides and vacant lots throughout the United States.

It blooms from July through October.

WHAT EATS IT

Some people cook chicory as a vegetable. Some use the root to make a hot drink like coffee.

Be aware of changing weather.

WILD LILY OF THE VALLEY

WHAT IT LOOKS LIKE

Wild lily of the valley plants grow about 6 inches tall on a zig-zag stem.

There are usually 2 leaves, sometimes 3, spaced along the stem. They are about as long as your finger. The heart-shaped end wraps around the stem. The other end is pointed.

The white flowers form a small, starry cluster. Each flower has 4 petals, each less than 1/4 inch long and wide. They have no smell.

Look for it in the midwestern United States eastward to the Atlantic coast and south to Georgia. The flowers bloom from May to July.

WHERE TO FIND IT

The plant likes moist woods and brushy areas where the soil is loose and deep. It often forms a dense mat, especially under trees.

INTERESTING FACTS

This wildflower is sometimes known as "mayflower" because the plant blooms in springtime.

WHAT EATS IT

Chipmunks, mice and grouse eat the pale, speckled berries. Rabbits eat the plants.

Stay away from poison ivy and poison oak when you explore.

ORANGE HAWKWEED

WHAT IT LOOKS LIKE

Orange hawkweed grows to 2 feet tall. The single stalk has dark hair on it. Several blooms grow at the very top.

Orange hawkweed flowers have yellow centers with a deep orange fringe around the outside. The petals look square with blunt ends that are ragged. The entire flower looks fringed. It is about the size of a bottle cap.

The leaves, which are hairy and coarse, grow only in a circle at the base of the stem. They are about the size of your thumb.

WHERE TO FIND IT

There are about 50 different kinds of hawkweeds that grow across the United States in fields, meadows, roadsides and lawns. They bloom from summer through early autumn.

When several hawkweed buds are open on the stalk, the plant has a sweet smell.

WHAT EATS IT

Grouse and wild turkeys eat the leaves and seeds. Deer, rabbits and mountain sheep eat the plants.

INTERESTING FACTS

Some people call this plant "devil's paintbrush" because it sometimes grows where people don't want it to grow.

When gathering common wildflowers, take only what you need and leave the others.

EVENING LYCHNIS

WHAT IT LOOKS LIKE

Evening lychnis flowers look like a green-striped, or purple-striped bag with petals sticking out of the closed top. Each single white flower, with its 5 deeply notched petals, grows at the end of each branched stem. There are 5 threads that poke up from the center.

The plant is hairy and the stems are slender. It grows from 1 to 2 feet tall with thin, sticky branches going every which way.

Its downy green leaves close around the stem and make a point at the other end. They are small and slender, about 2 inches long. The undersides are paler green than the tops.

WHERE TO FIND IT

Evening lychnis is widespread across the eastern United States, although it can be found throughout most of the United States. It likes places like vacant lots and roadsides.

These flowers are closed during the day. They have a faint, fresh scent. Look for the blossoms all summer and into early fall.

WHAT EATS IT

Sparrows eat the seeds. Moths like the flowers.

INTERESTING FACTS

Evening lychnis blossoms open at night when moths can pollinate them.

34

When exploring at night, take a flashlight.

COMMON MILKWEED

WHAT IT LOOKS LIKE

Milkweeds grow to 5 feet tall, and usually have just 1 stem per plant.

The leathery, oval leaves of the common milkweed are smooth and about 6 inches long and 4 inches wide. They are fuzzy underneath.

The flowers look rubbery. Each clump is about the size of a golf ball, and can be white, red-orange or pink-violet.

WHERE TO FIND IT

These plants don't like to be crowded by other kinds of wildflowers. Instead, they usually grow by themselves in a patch. Some kinds of milkweed grow almost everywhere across the United States.

They may be found in fields, meadows, woods or swamps, or along roadsides. You can find them blooming from early to late summer.

WHAT EATS IT

This is a special plant to Monarch butterflies. Some birds also eat milkweed seeds. Antelopes eat the plants. Spicy, sweet-smelling milkweed flowers attract flies, bees and butterflies.

INTERESTING FACTS

This wildflower gets its name from the milky juice in its sturdy stems.

Tell an adult where you are going, or take one with you.

VIRGINIA BLUEBELL

WHAT IT LOOKS LIKE

Virginia bluebells grow from 1 to 2 feet tall on smooth stems. Virginia bluebell leaves are yellow-green and oval. They are smooth and can be longer than your hand.

The plant is named for its small bell-shaped flowers. They are blue, about 1 inch long, and grow in clusters.

The blossoms have a faint, fresh scent while they are blooming in April and May.

WHERE TO FIND IT

They like rich soil and shady places, such as the woods near rivers and other bottomlands. Look for Virginia bluebells in the eastern United States and along the upper Great Lakes as far west as northern Minnesota.

WHAT EATS IT

Wildlife do not usually eat Virginia bluebells.

INTERESTING FACTS

Look closely at the buds. The flowers are blue, but the buds are pink!

Never hurt any wildflowers with your hands or tools.

INDIAN PAINTBRUSH

WHAT IT LOOKS LIKE

Indian paintbrush flowers are small. Each one looks like an upended paintbrush covered with red and yellow color. The flower grows at the end of the stem.

Each flower is really a group of short, 2-lipped flowers that are yellow-green. You can easily see the taller, 3-part sections that are tipped with red. The yellow-green flowers are nearly hidden beneath them.

The stem is hairy and straight. The few leaves along its length are shaped like thin, bristly pitchforks. They are about 2 inches long.

There is also a circle of leaves around the base of the plant on the ground. These are oval and up to 3 inches long.

INTERESTING FACTS

Although they have good roots, they sometimes attach themselves to other plant roots for easy food.

WHERE TO FIND IT

This wildflower grows from 1 to 2 feet tall in vacant lots, roadsides and meadows. It is found throughout the eastern United States, south to the Gulf Coast and west into the Great Plains.

They bloom during late spring and early summer. They have no smell.

WHAT EATS IT

Deer and wild mules eat the plants. Hummingbirds enjoy the flowers.

Don't approach or touch any wild animals you may see.

Make a Container Rainbow

No matter where you live, you can plant and enjoy a rainbow of color.

WHAT YOU NEED

▼

- A clean, empty ice cream bucket with a few holes punched in the bottom
- Garden soil
- Seeds of any of the short, easy-to-grow wildflowers in this book, such as orange hawkweed, coneflower, and white clover
- A watering can

Butterflies love plants such as milkweed, wild rose and Queen Anne's Lace. You will be amazed how quickly they come when the flowers begin to bloom!

something to do

WHAT TO DO

▼

1 Fill the ice cream bucket with the garden soil.

2 Lightly press the wildflower seeds into the soil. Remember that in the wild, seeds often lay near the top of the ground.

3 Water the top of the soil to moisten it. Do not make it soggy.

4 Set the bucket in a warm, sunny place. Water the soil as needed to keep it moist.

5 After a few weeks, the seeds should sprout. Continue to water the bucket as the seeds grow into a rainbow of flowers for you to enjoy.

If you have a place outdoors, you can plant a wildflower garden to attract butterflies. A sunny, unused corner of your yard or garden works very well. It can be as big or little as you wish.

ice cream

For More Information

MORE BOOKS TO READ

Into the Woods: A Woodland Scrapbook. Loretta Krupinski (HarperCollins)
The Nature and Science of Flowers. Exploring the Science of Nature series. Jane Burton
    and Kim Taylor (Gareth Stevens)
The Science of Plants. Living Science series. Jonathan Bocknek (Gareth Stevens)
What's Your Favorite Flower? Allen Fowler (Children's Press)
Wildflowers Around the World. Elaine Landay (Watts)
Wildflowers: A Garden Primer. Anne Velghe (Farrer)

VIDEOS

The Children's Garden Project. (Video 11)
Flower Magic: Flower Safari. (Dancing Wave Music)
Look What I Grew: Windowsill Gardens. (Library Video)
The Magic School Bus: Goes to Seed. (WarnerVision)
The Plant World. (United Learning)
Science Essentials: Plants. (Encyclopædia Britannica Education Corporation)

WEB SITES

www.mmcinc.com/wildflowers/home.asp
www.wildflower.org/

Some web sites stay current longer than others. For further web sites, use your search engines to locate the following topics: *flowers, gardening, seeds, wildflowers,* and *wildlife habitat.*

INDEX